What is

Kiss My Ass

The Vulgar and Delightful Adult Coloring book

By

S.B. Nozaz

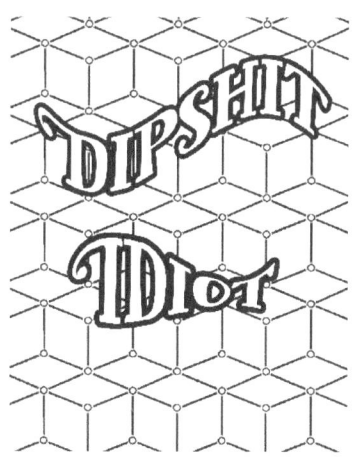

ATTENTION WHORE

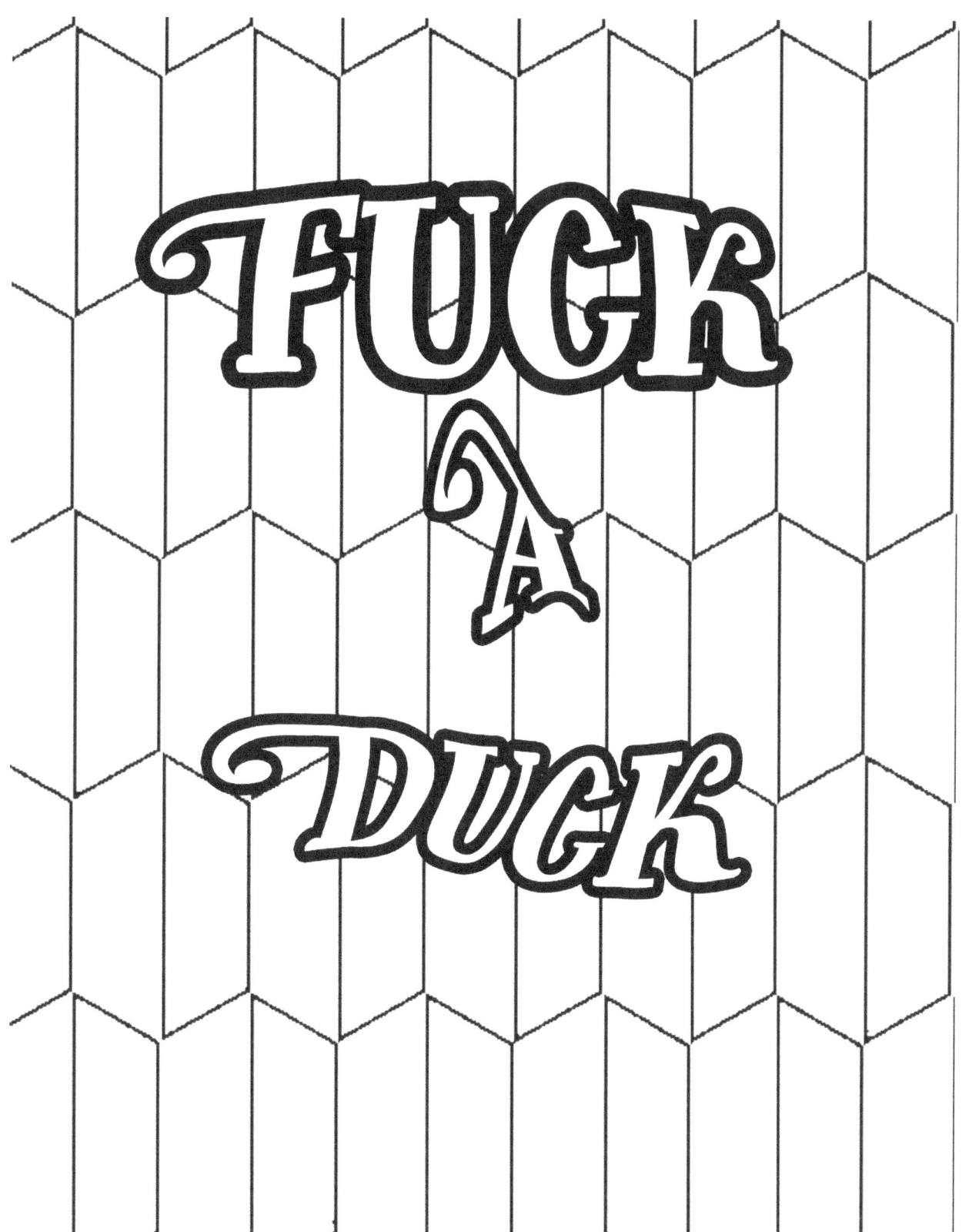

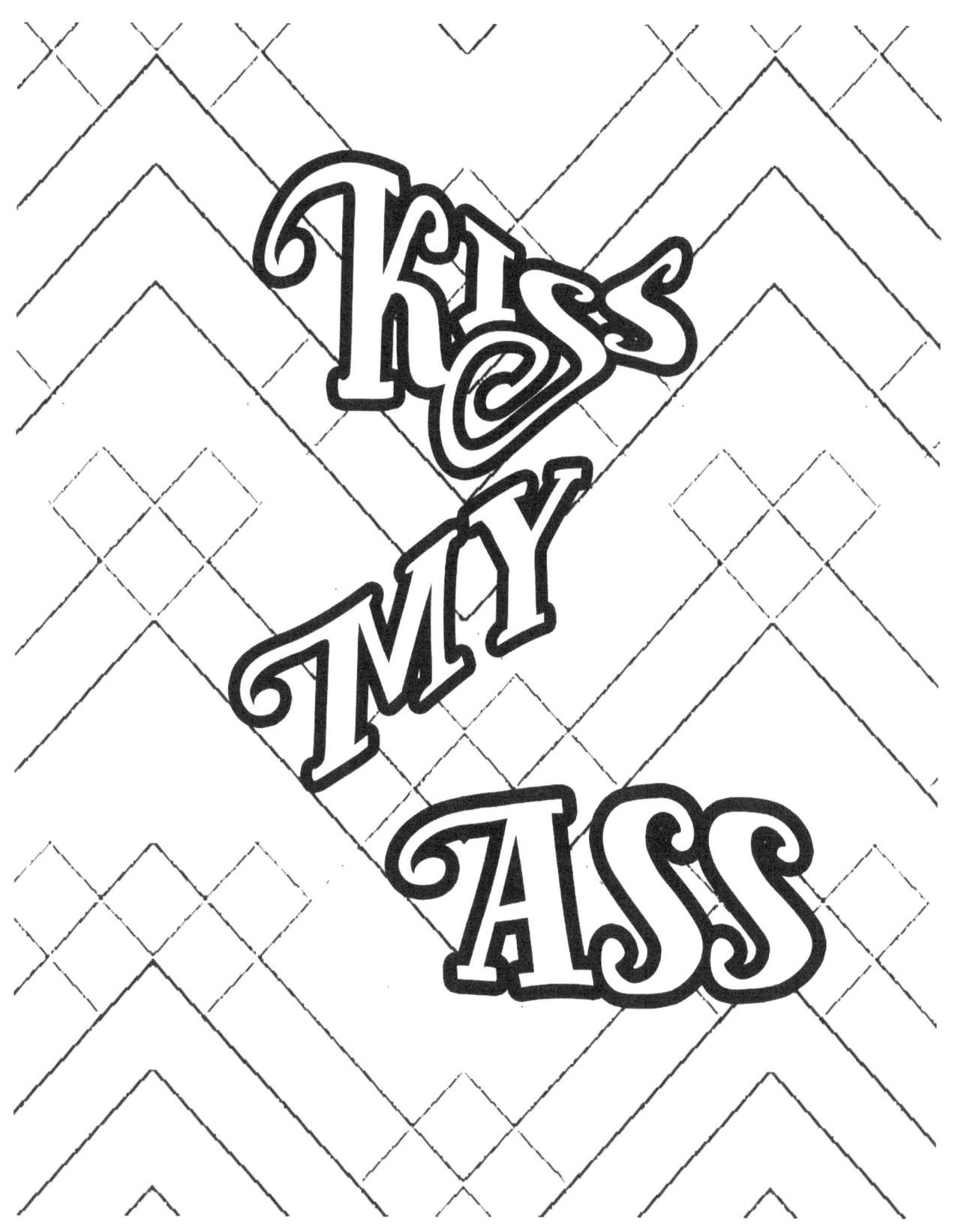

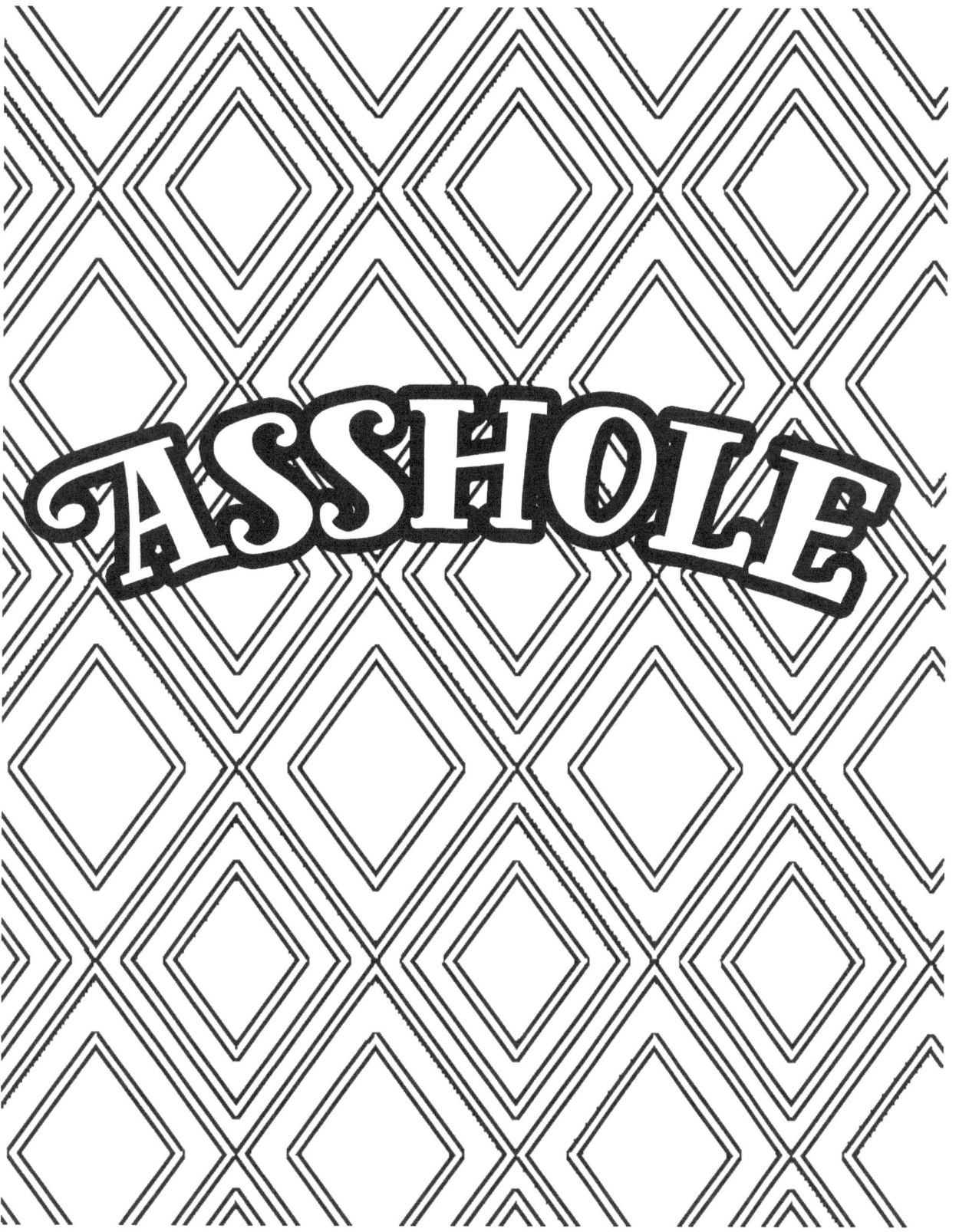

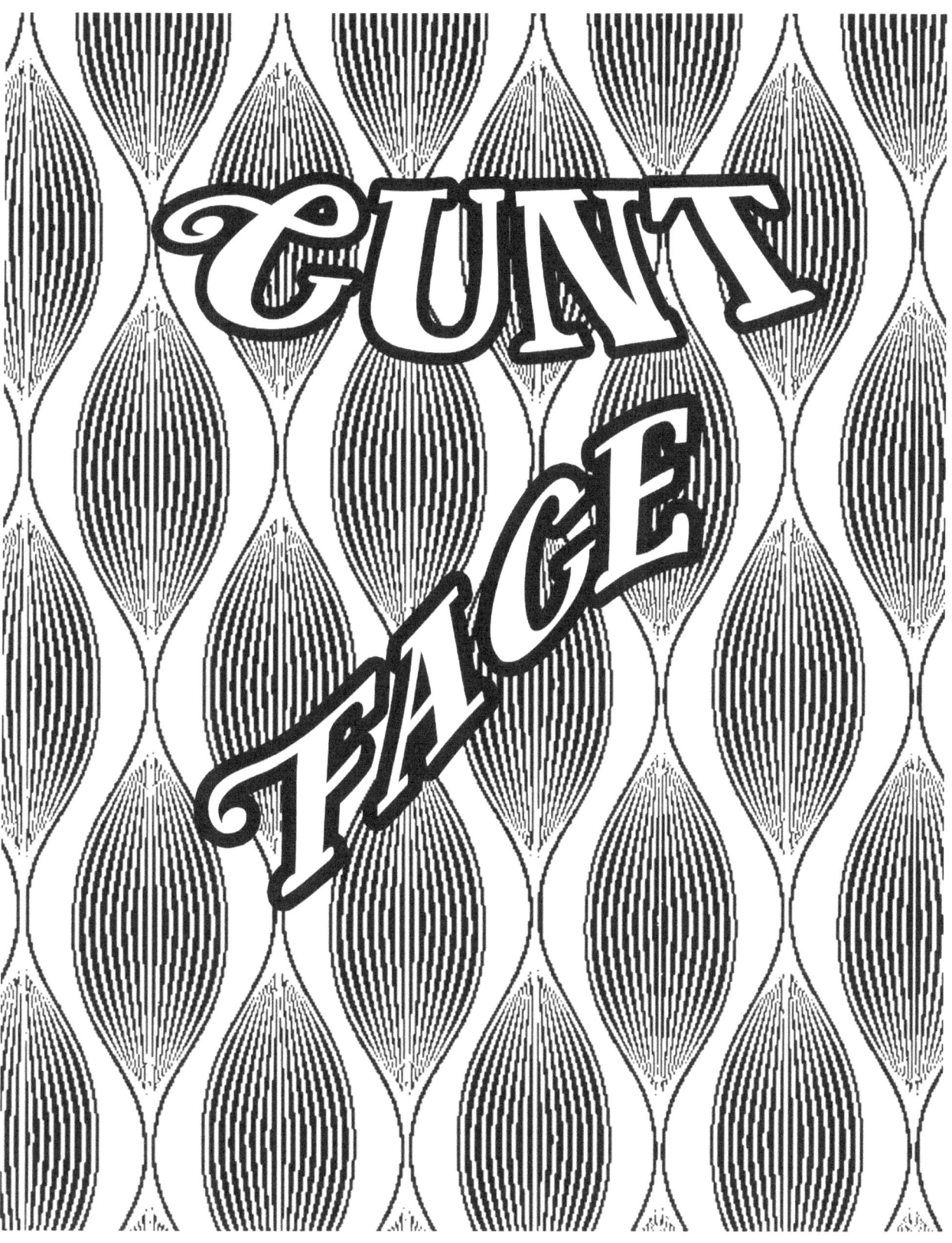

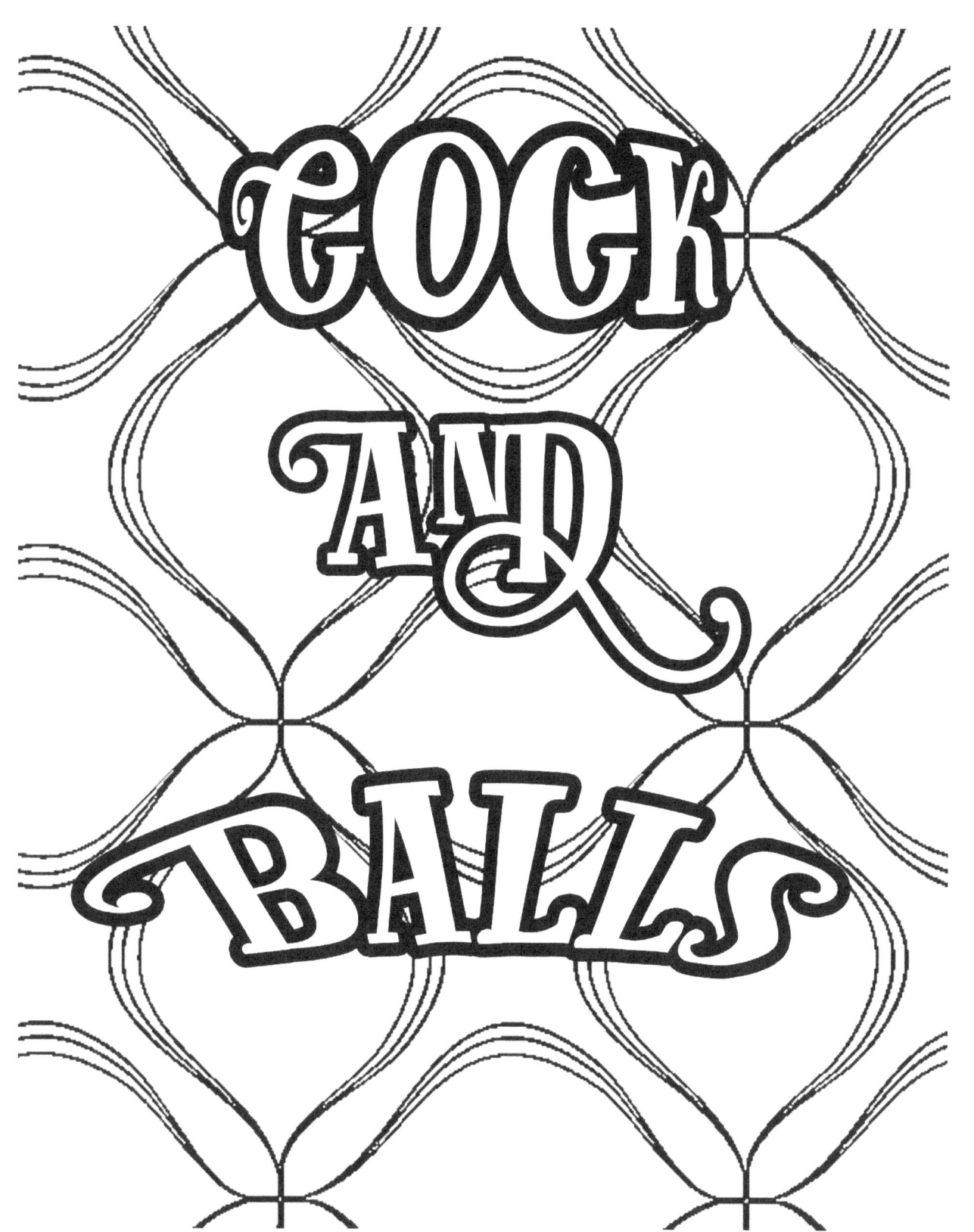

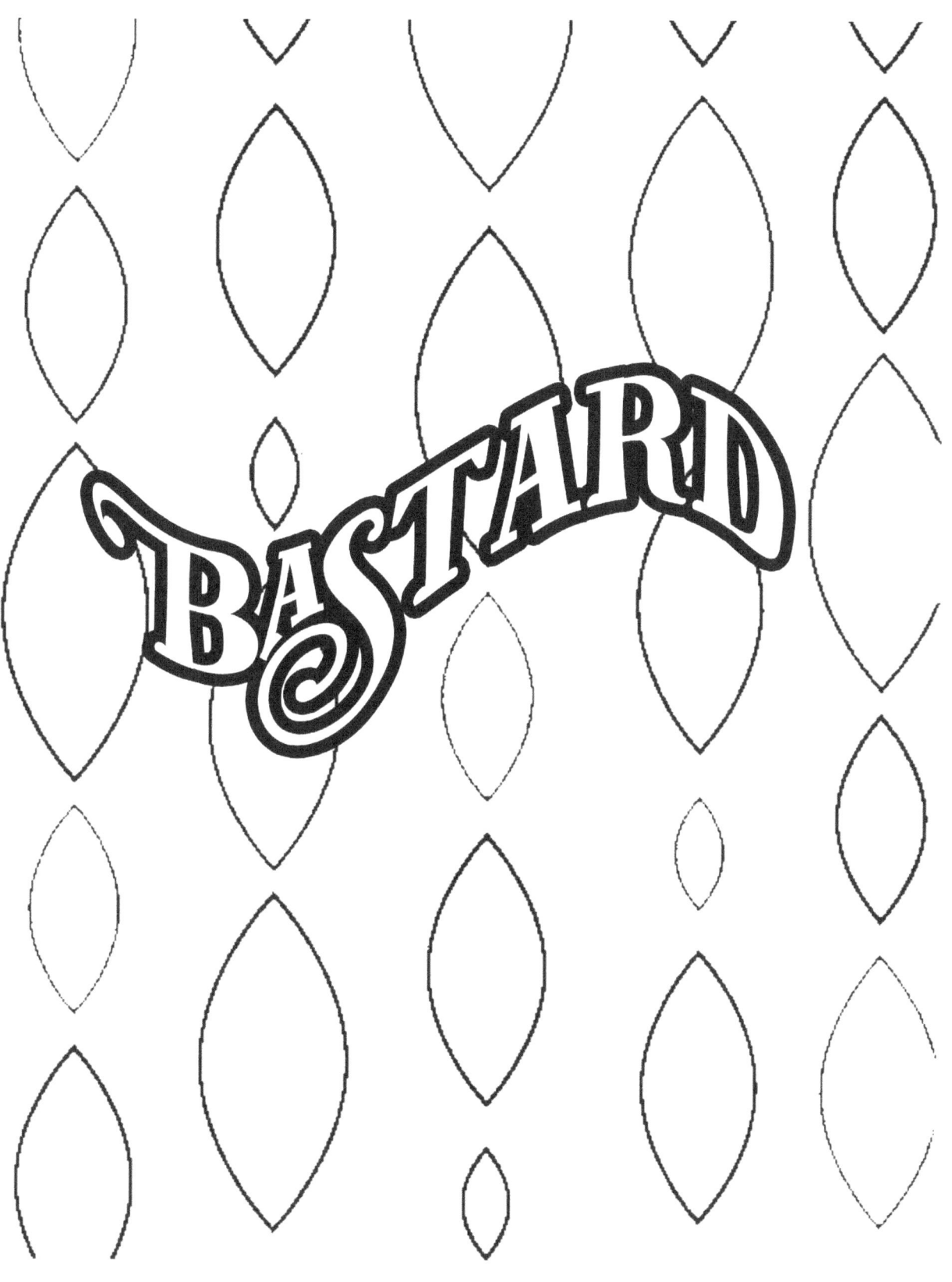

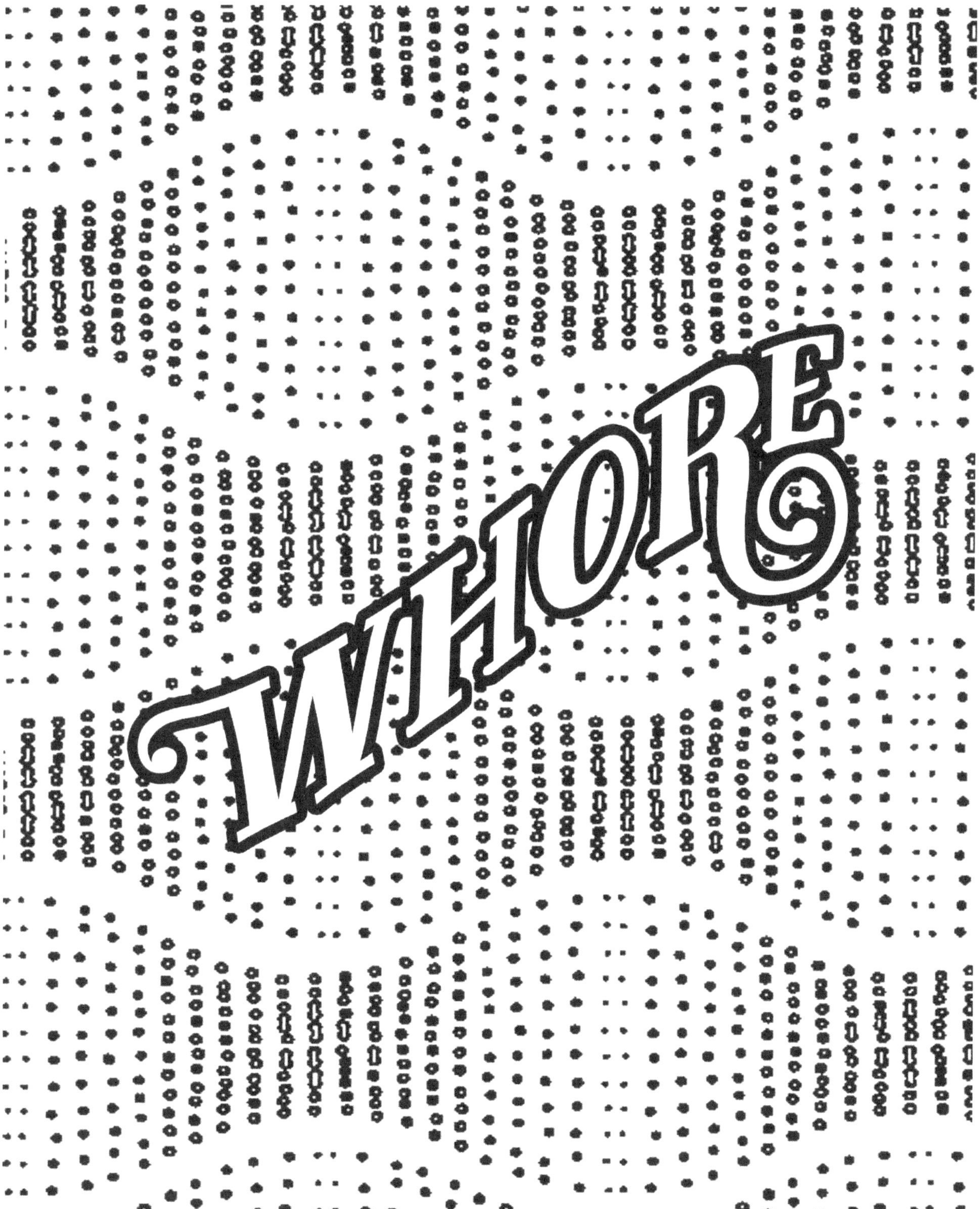

BATSHIT CRAZY

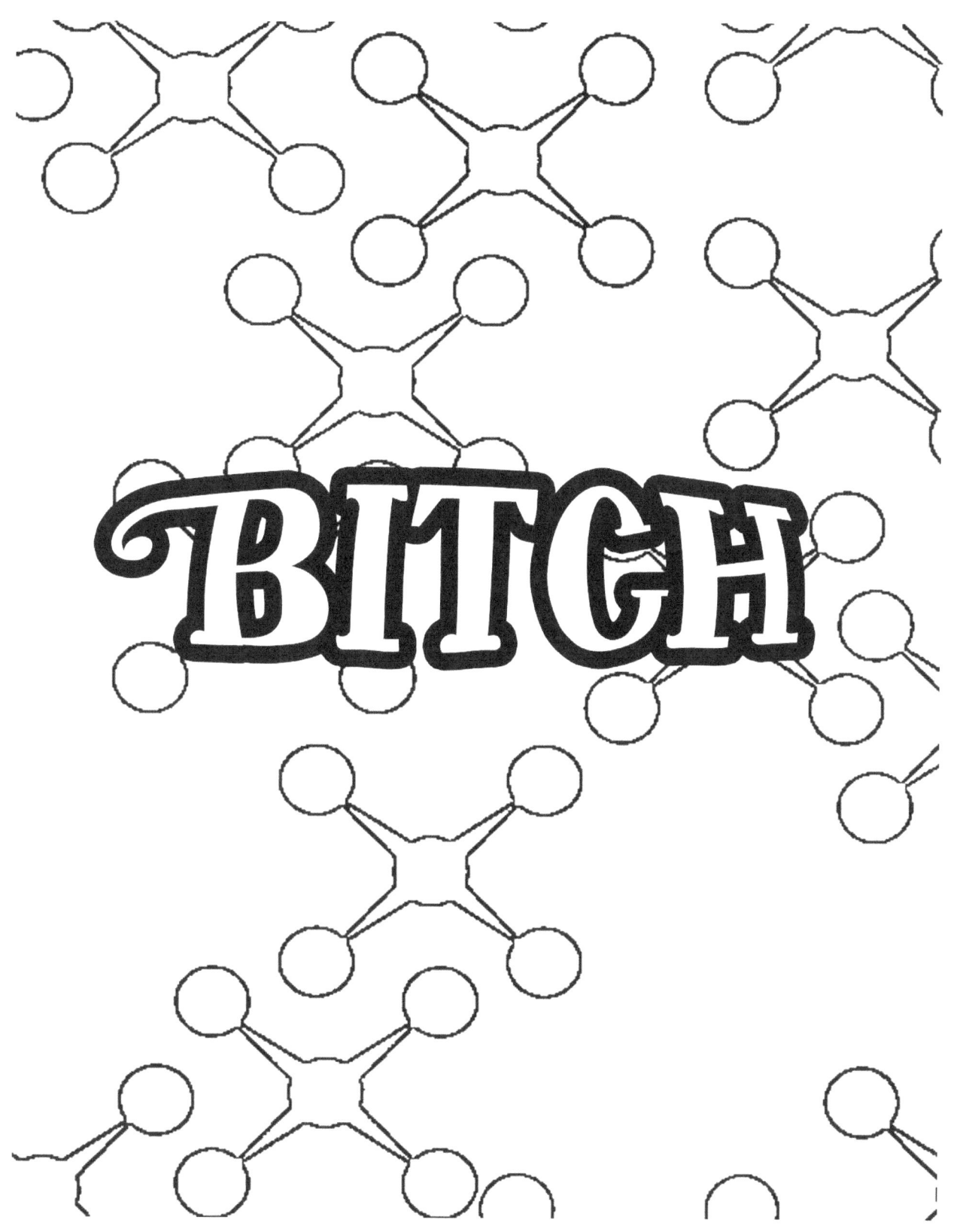

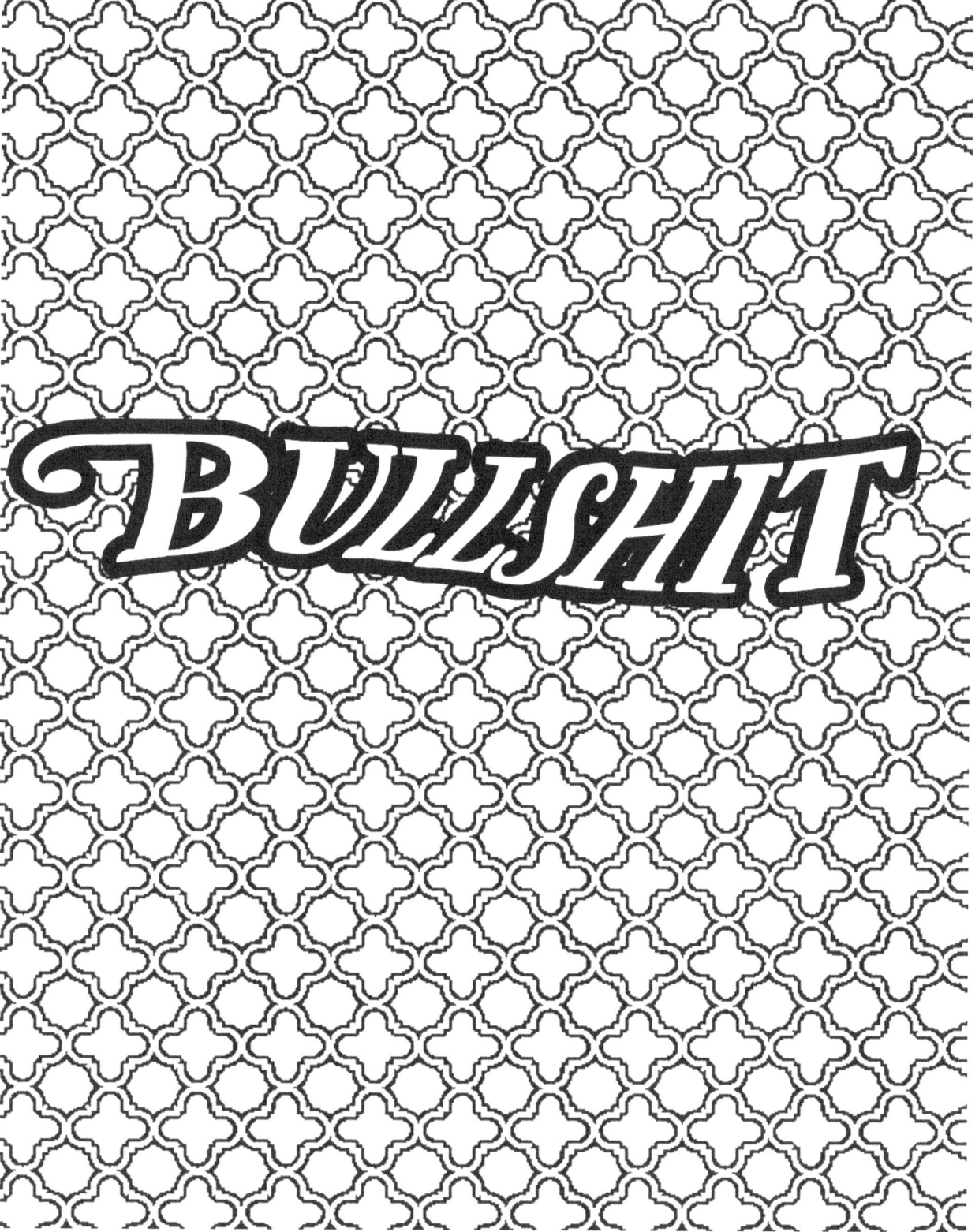

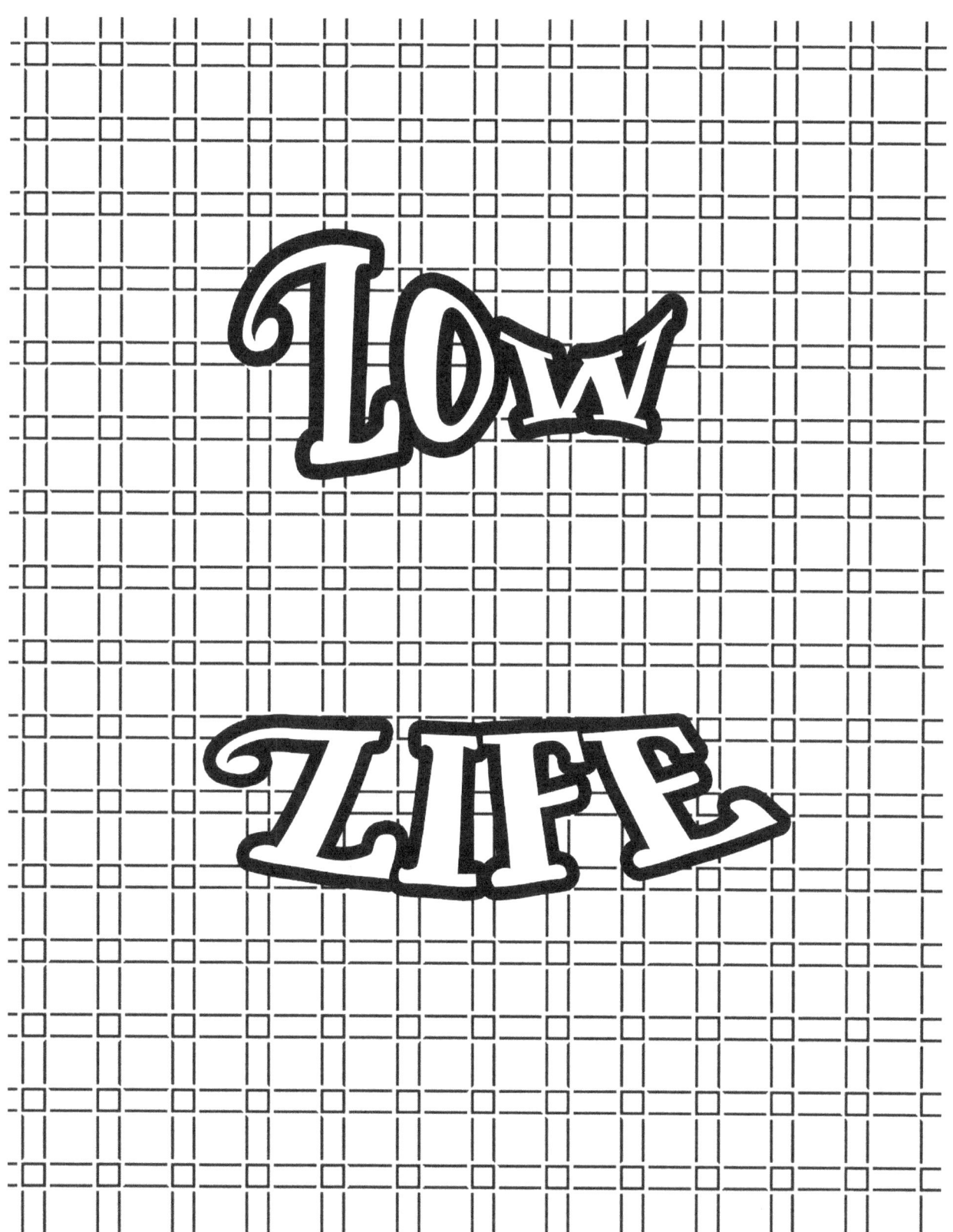

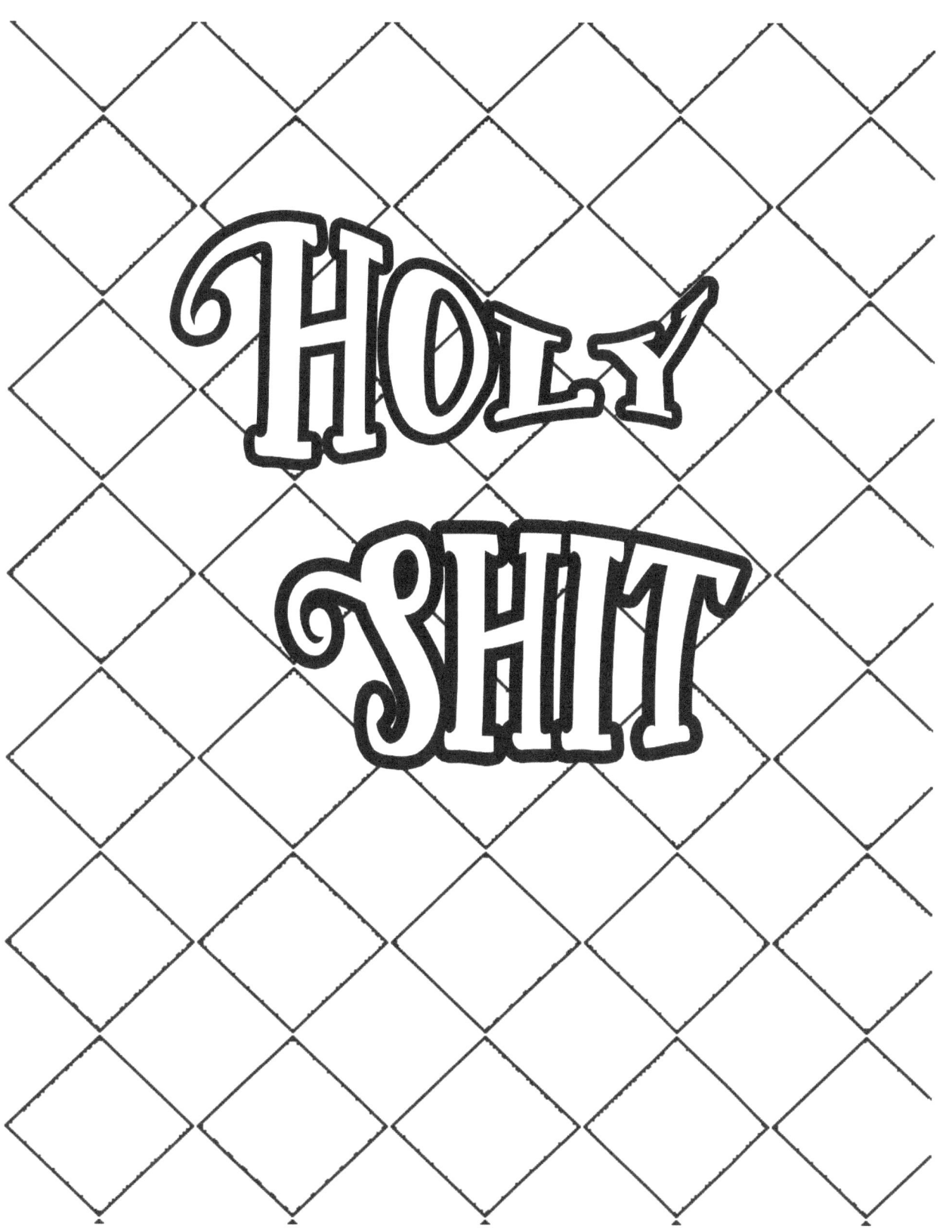

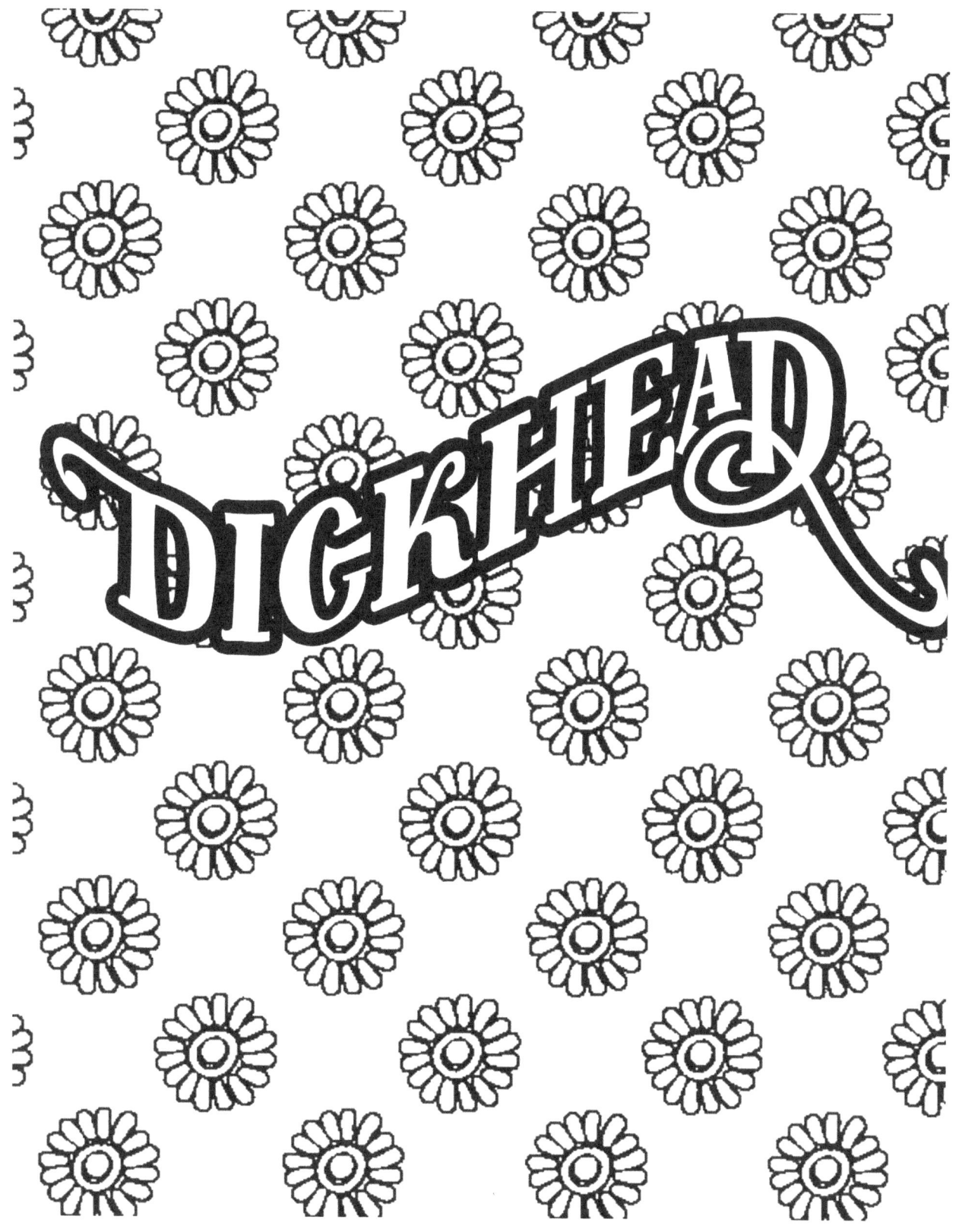

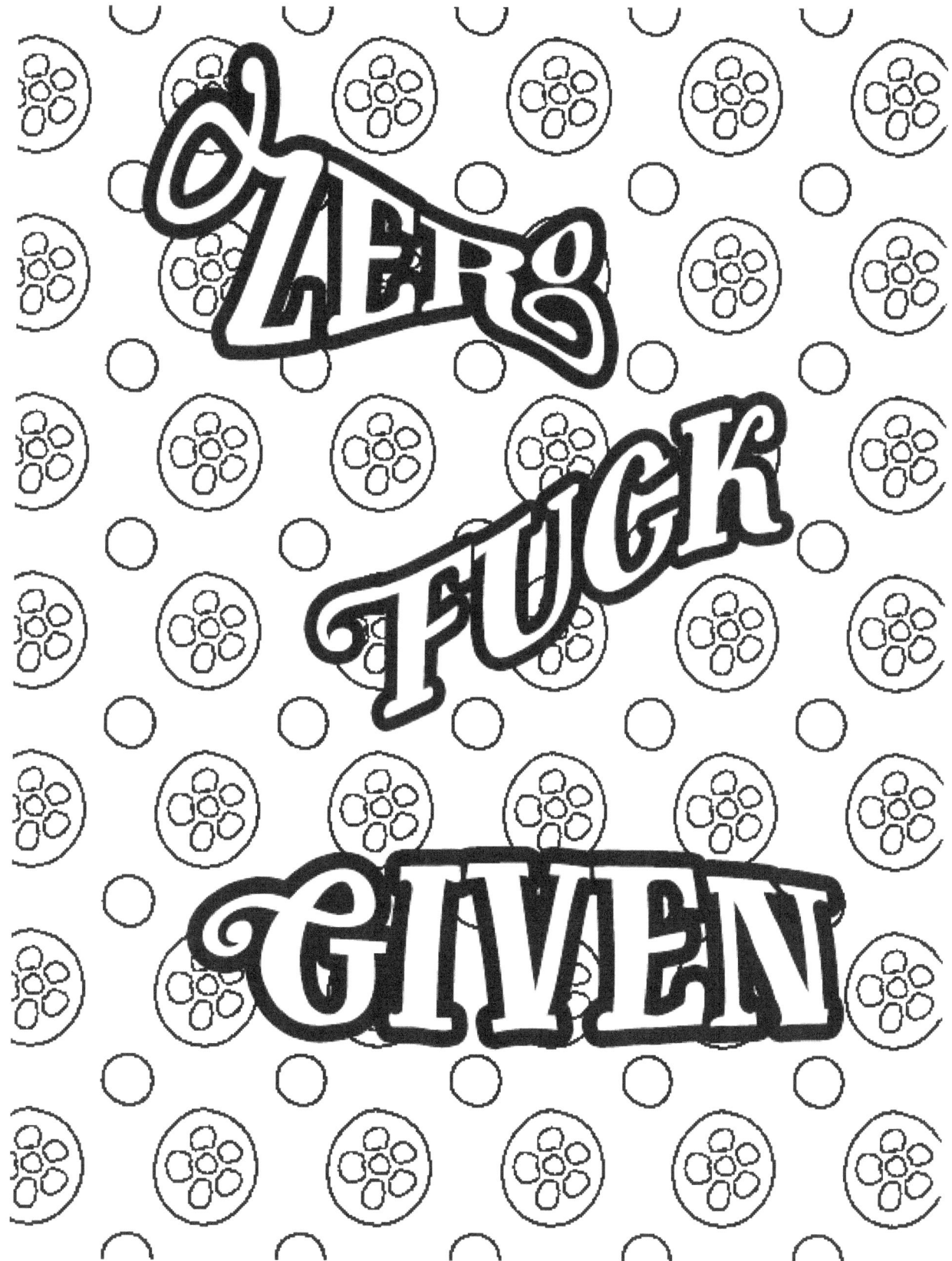

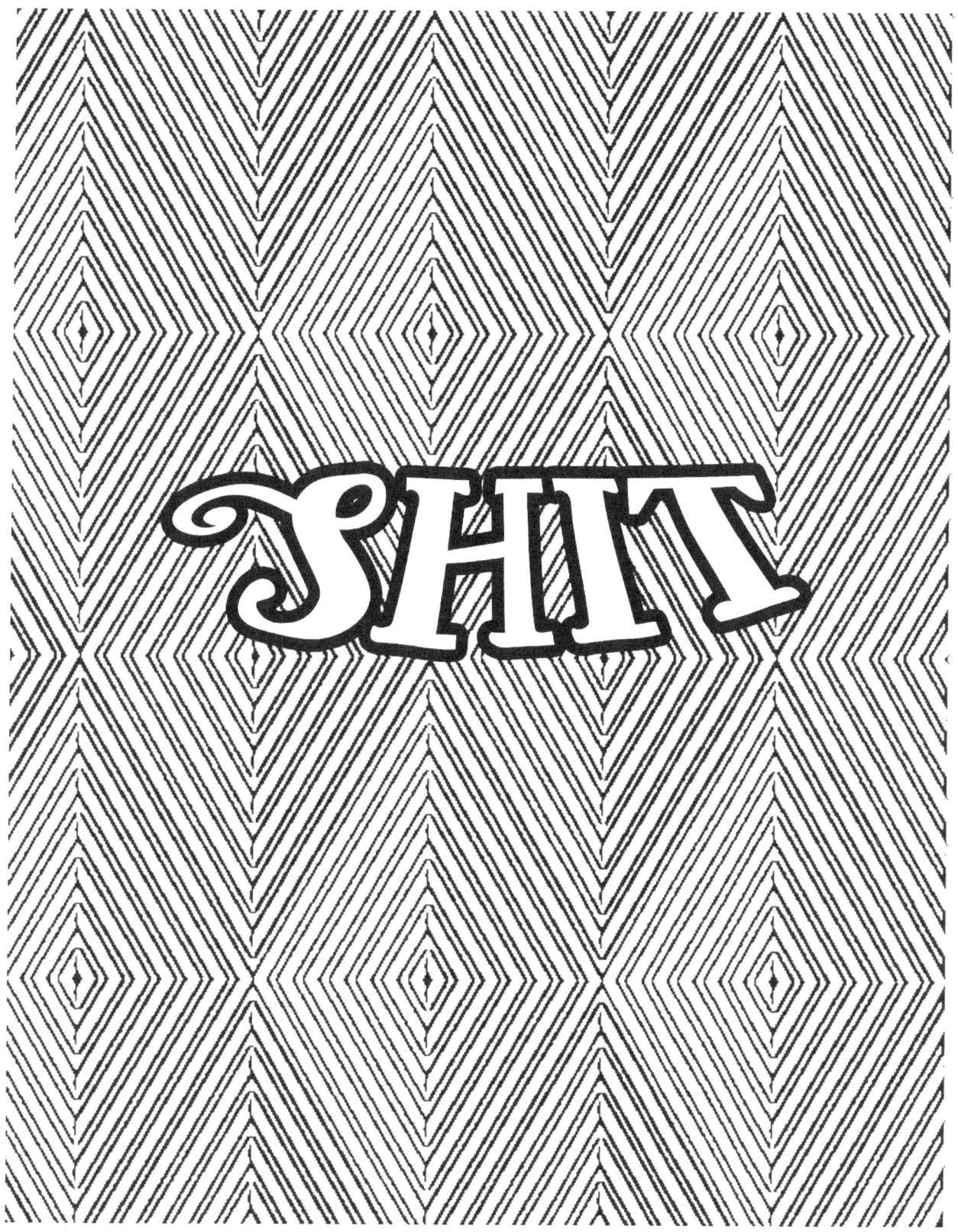

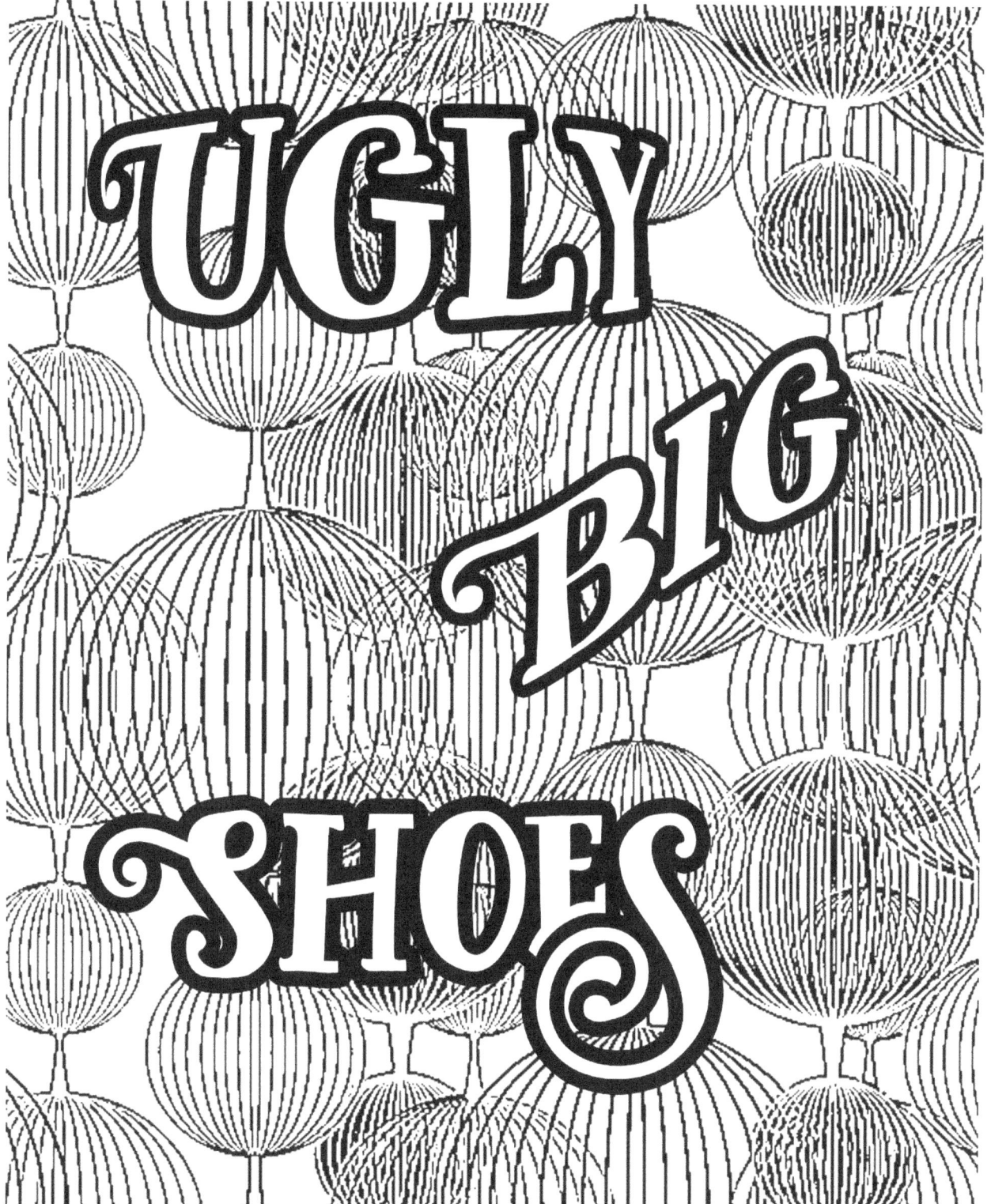

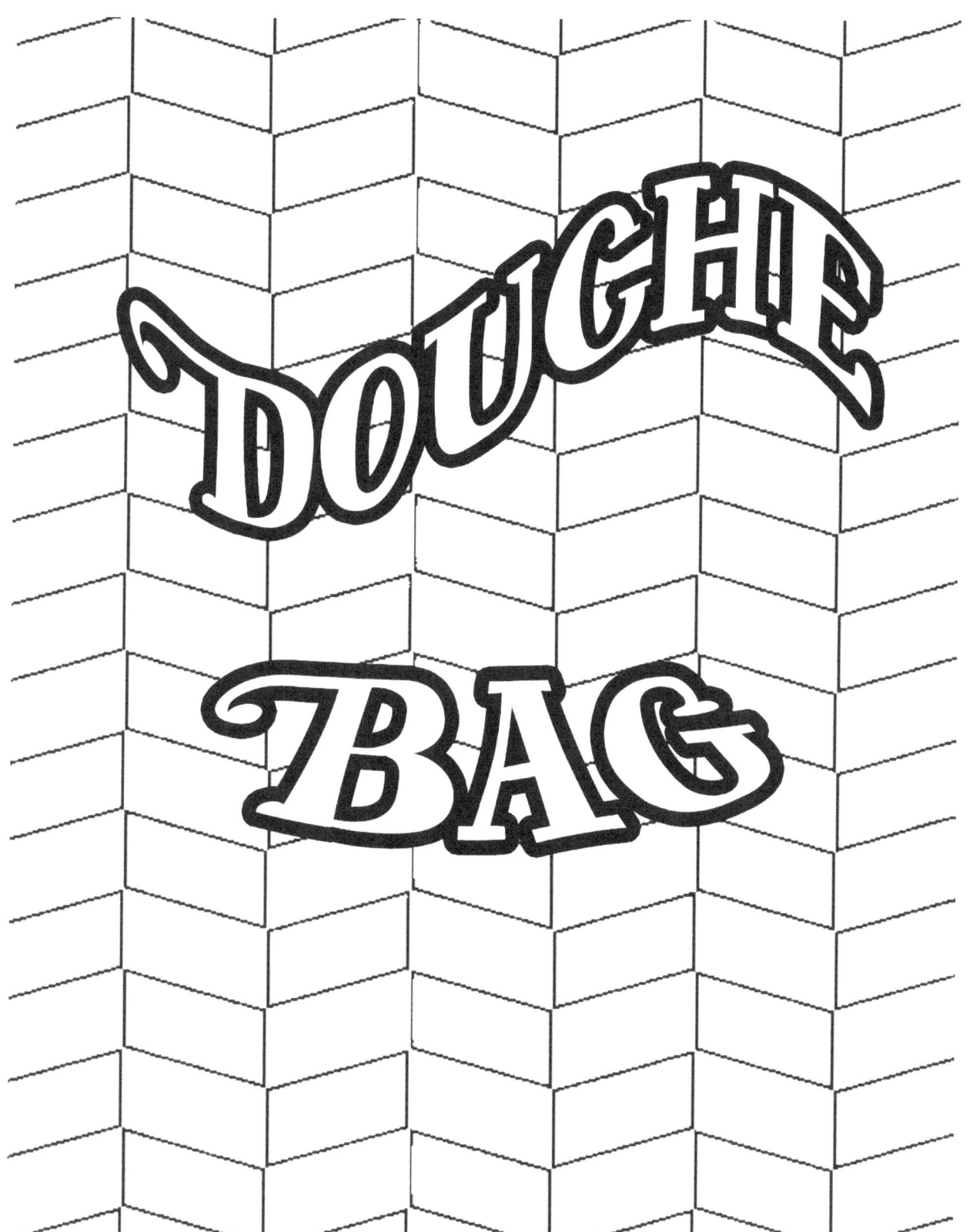

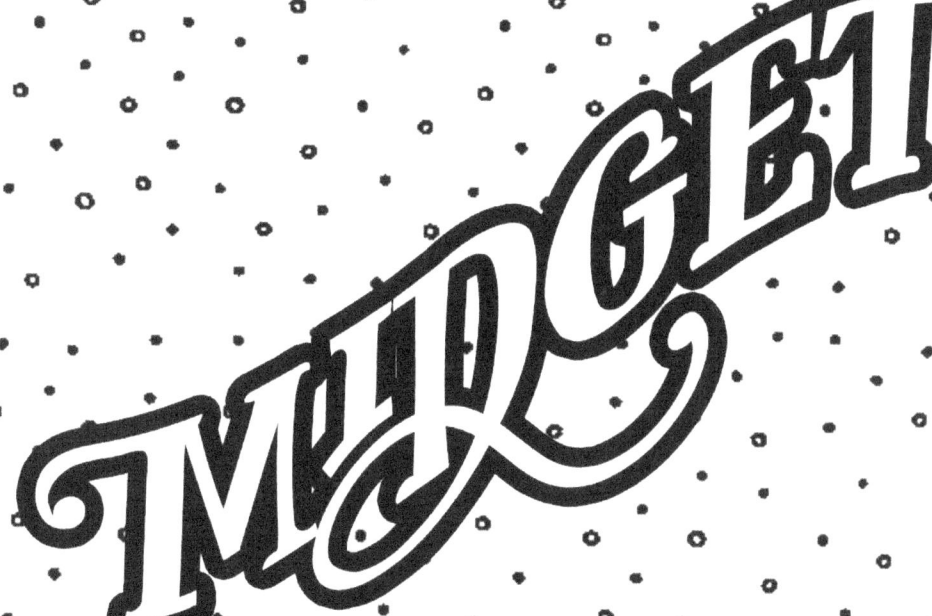

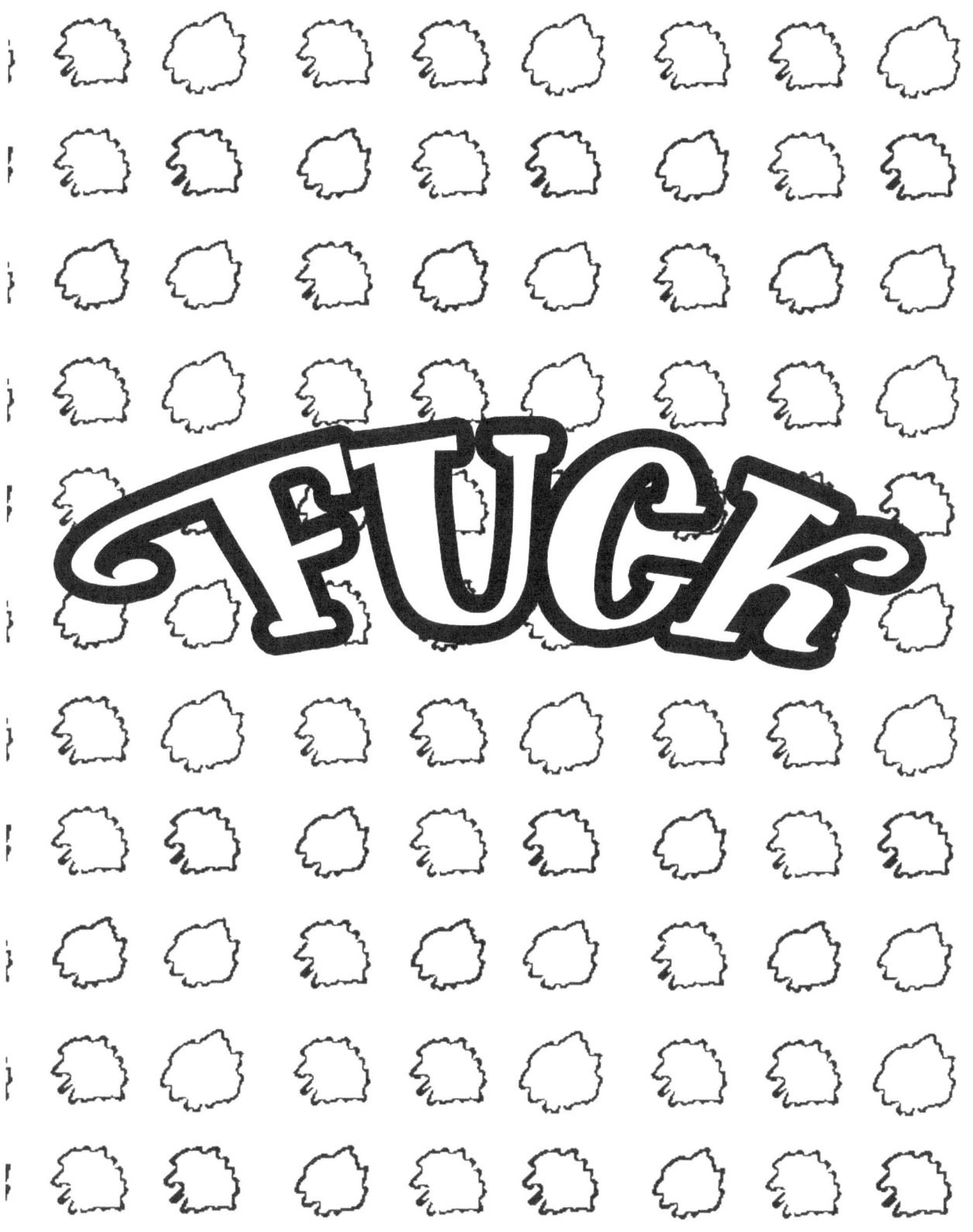

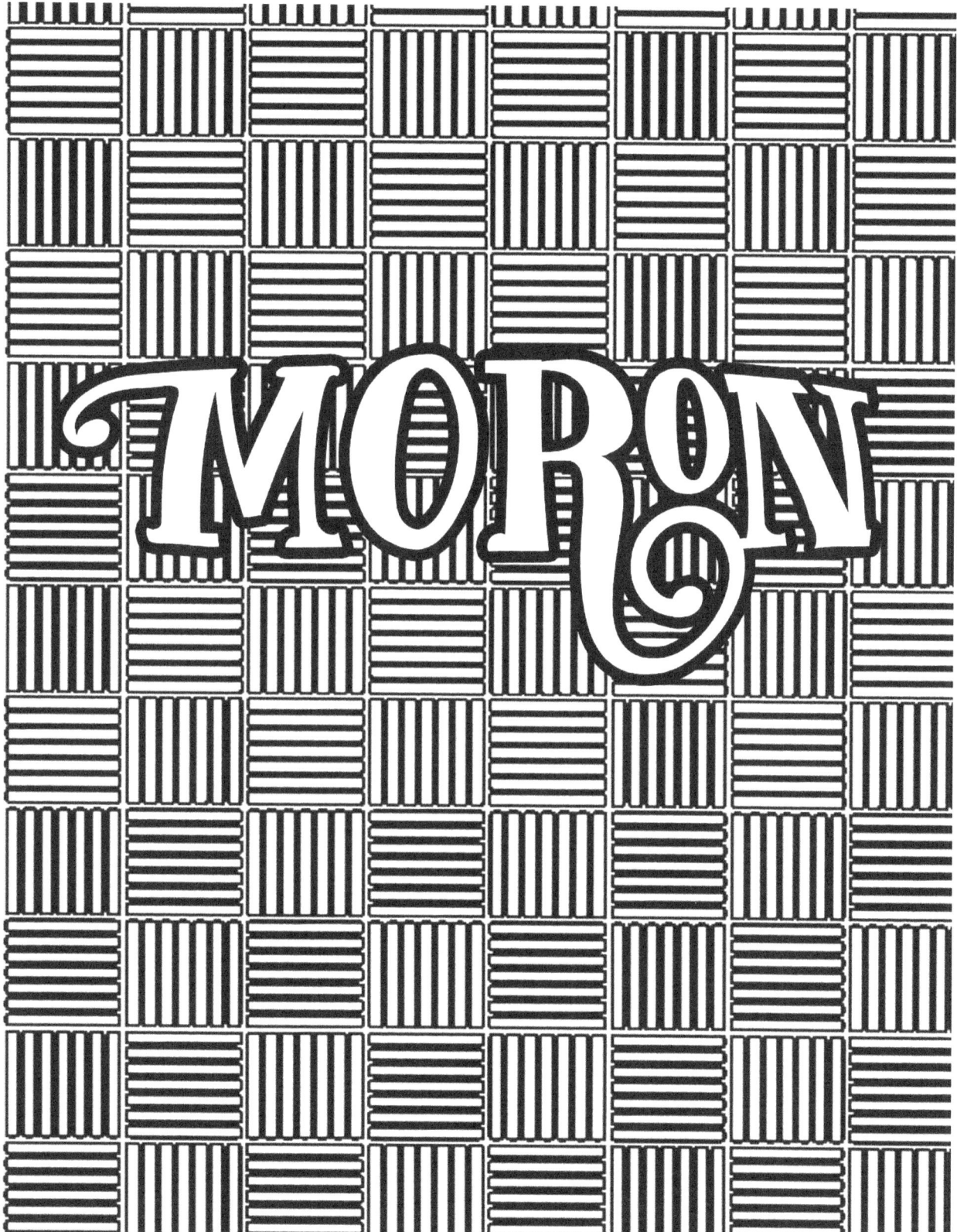

HOLLY FUCK

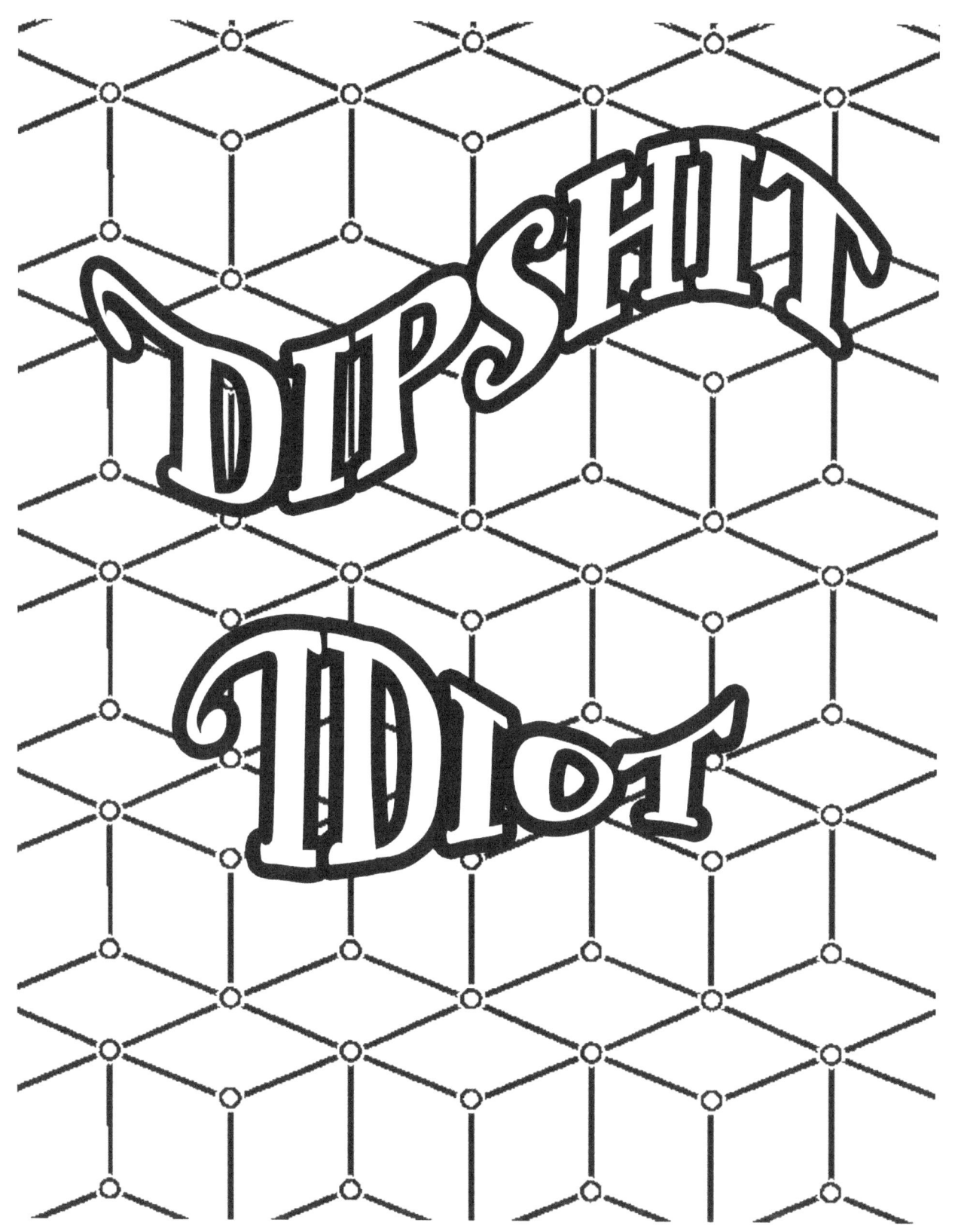

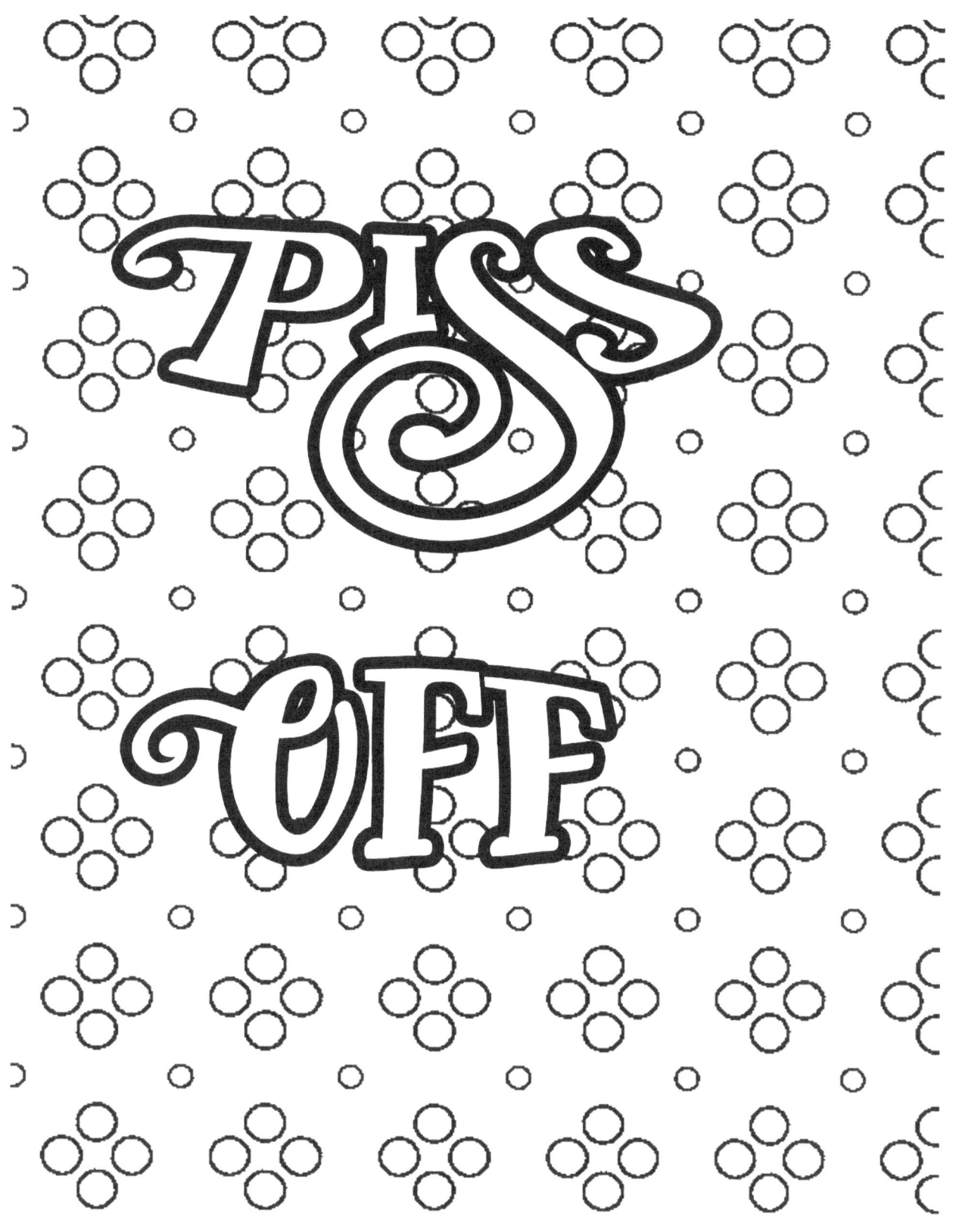

Note

www.ingramcontent.com/pod-product-compliance
Lightning Source LLC
Chambersburg PA
CBHW080639190526
45169CB00009B/3433